UNIVERSE OF FASHION

YvesSaintLaurent

By Pierre Bergé

UNIVERSE / VENDOME

First published in the United States of America in 1997
by UNIVERSE PUBLISHING
A Division of Rizzoli International Publications, Inc.
300 Park Avenue South
New York, NY 10010

and THE VENDOME PRESS

Copyright © 1997 Éditions Assouline, Paris
English translation copyright © 1997 Thames and Hudson, London

Front cover: Shirt jacket and cotton gabardine waistcoat.
Yves Saint Laurent Rive Gauche. Summer 1996.
Photo Mario Testino. © Archives Yves Saint Laurent.
Back cover: Wedding dress in purple and black iridescent faille.
Winter 1981. Photo Arthur Elgort.

ISBN 0-7893-0067-2

Printed and bound it Italy

Library of Congress Catalog Card Number: 97-060145

Foreword

In 1957, when Christian Dior died, Yves Saint Laurent took over as designer for the house of Dior. In 1962, Yves Saint Laurent presented his first collection under his own label, and the house that he built was to become an empire. Here is the story of Yves Saint Laurent, the designer, as told by Pierre Bergé, his partner.

Yves Saint Laurent changed the beat of fashion. It is not enough to sum up his career simply by recalling his trademark "looks"—the blouson, the pants, the see-through tops, the smoking, the safari clothes, the leather look. What about the memorable Russian Collection in 1976, or the collections that showed us Yves's eye on Mondrian, on the Cubists, on pop art? And then there was the great stir caused by his masculin-féminin tailored pantsuit. Let there be no confusion, though, for in a Saint Laurent pantsuit—as in any of his designs—women always looked like women. Those of us who attended his showings remember the relief of being able to stop our note-taking momentarily as one number passed that was not quite as good as the twenty that came before it—a "weak" item that, by any other standard, would probably have been a star.

"Fashion," writes Bergé, "is art if it is made by an artist." To Bergé, there were Sunday painters and Wednesday couturiers. Yves Saint Laurent was neither. In fact, his Wednesday morning showings put the previous days' collections into perspective. Yves Saint Laurent was recreating fashion week by week. He could single-handedly rescue a poor week of showings, and he made a good week memorable. Yves Saint Laurent was defining the clothes women wore: from the suit that opened his show to the see-through number that closed it. New life was breathed into fashion all over the world.

How fortunate were those who saw that first Dior collection designed by Saint Laurent. How fortunate those who first wore his clothes. How fortunate for all that Yves Saint Laurent had the passion to unite his remarkable talents—his extraordinary color sense, his passion for theatre, his love of painting—under the single overarching belief that "Clothes must be at the service of women."

The day—if it comes—that Yves Saint Laurent announces his last couture line may not mark the end of haute couture, but it will hail the end of an era. And while the world will ultimately decide whether Saint Laurent is a genius, few will argue that he is truly one of the great masters.

Grace Mirabella

Preface

October 30th 1957, Montaroux in the Var area of France. In a newspaper photograph of the crowd around Christian Dior's coffin, two young men may be seen standing a short distance apart. They did not yet know each other but fate was soon to bring them together. These two men were Yves Saint Laurent and Pierre Bergé. I have always considered our being photographed together unawares as an omen. If either of us had been told what our lives were to become, we would not have believed it. Our presence beside Dior's coffin was pure chance. But is there such a thing as chance, or could it just be fate upsetting the rules of the game and inventing new ones? We were young. Yves had just turned twenty-one, I was nearly twenty-seven. When I think back to those days, I am always astonished how sure we were of ourselves. Although we never said it, we were convinced that the whole world was within our grasp. Everything happened so fast.

Yves went to hospital whilst doing his military service; he lost his job at Dior; I was chosen to pass on the news, and it was at the Val-de-Grâce hospital that we took the decision to open a couture house together. All we lacked was the money. But the immense faith I had in Yves' talent gave me the strength I needed and encouraged me to throw caution to the winds. Indeed, one had to be reckless to want to open a couture house and build an empire without a penny. But that was our dream. Dior was the model we wished to rival and surpass. Neither Yves nor I could have imagined all that awaited us, but from the very first day we were driven by an urge to succeed which has never left us. Our story is essentially that of our couture house. We have lived at its rhythm, with its inverted seasons where winter collections are presented in the height of summer and those of summer in mid-winter. However, nothing will ever replace that first collection presented on January 29th 1962. Everything was at stake that day. The day we set out on our adventure, riddled with nerves and anxiety. The day Yves won his first battle. From that moment onwards I understood that this proud young general of all of twenty-five was going to lead us from victory to victory. From that moment onwards I realized that for many years to come I would preside over the company we had so longed for, and that, at Yves' side, I in turn would become a leader. Then as now, rallying under our banner designed by Cassandre, Yves and I would fight numerous battles which through Yves' miraculous talent alone we always won. The years have passed by, battles have followed battles, but our enthusiasm has never waned and, from time to time, at dawn, on the eve of a collection, when robes are still coming down from the sewing rooms, I imagine myself transported back to that fateful day in January 1962.

How much have we changed over all these years? A great deal, no doubt. But what does that matter? We have done so much! We have accomplished something beyond the wildest dreams of our youth. As for Yves, he has written one of the finest pages in the history of French genius. He should be a happy man. But to believe this would be to forget that creation is always the union of both talent and suffering. ■

I s fashion an art? The question has often been asked over the last few years and not about fashion alone. Like cinema, painting, music, literature and poetry, fashion is an art when practised by an artist. In the same way that there are 'Sunday painters' there are 'Sunday couturiers' and we should not be surprised that there are so many of them. In a century which has seen the advent of so many different forms of expression, we can surely refer to fashion as Art. When Marcel Duchamp presents a bottle rack or a urinal, has he created a work of art? I am not entirely sure. What I am sure of is that Duchamp is an artist in the same way that Chanel, Schiaparelli, Vionnet, Dior, Balenciaga and Saint Laurent are. I will concede that they may be more fragile, more ephemeral, but there is no denying that their work is creation. It would be ridiculous, and above all, reactionary in this day and age, to refuse the status of artists to creators of fashion. Can we reject primitive, tribal art? The admirable African exhibition at the Royal Academy in London in 1995 immediately addressed the subject in its title 'The Art of a Continent'. There is no hint of ambiguity in this definition. When a couturier is an artist he creates a work of art.

Haute couture was born the day when women, tired of being subjected to the vagaries of fashion, demanded a set of rules to provide them with the reassurance they needed. *Haute couture* is not an end in itself. Creation in fashion cannot be abstract. Whatever may be said, ours is a profession conjugated in the present. Never in the past, never in the future. *Haute couture* only exists to be *lived*. It must share the lives of the women who wear it. Otherwise, however beautiful they may be, dresses will spend more time in suit sacks and closets than at glamorous dinners and parties. Life today has obviously changed. The civilization of 'being' is gradually replacing that of 'appearing'. Nowadays, there are very few real parties and dinners. It was not the Opera Bastille that sounded the death knell of the famous 'black tie evenings'; but the wind of change. None but a handful of the most nostalgic insist on dressing up to go to the opera, and it is immediately apparent that their hearts are no longer in it for they are fighting a rearguard action. *Haute couture* will not die for lack of creators or clients, but because the events, places or occasions permitting it to exist will have disappeared. Carriages have given way to taxis and those that remain only serve to transport tourists in search of the past. Let us spare *haute couture* this fate.

Over the last few years, fashion creation, so long associated with *haute couture*, has been drawing steadily closer to ready-to-wear and it is at this crossroads that we find Yves Saint Laurent. Ever vigilant, Yves Saint Laurent understood before any-one else that *haute couture* would mark time if it wasn't contemporary. This was the lesson to be learnt from Chanel. Like her, he appropriated signs and symbols from the world around him, transformed them and integrated them into the creative process. In this way he was to create black leather jackets, safari jackets, peajackets, tuxedos and the famous trouser-suits. All these clothes, and many others, enjoy enormous success throughout the world and will no doubt do so for many years to come.

Saint Laurent's advantage over Chanel has been the era he has lived through. He understood that fashion had to explore new horizons. He was the first couturier to open a ready-to-wear boutique independent of his couture house. This was in 1966, two years before May 1968 turned everything upside down. Nothing was to be the same again. Practically everyone else would plunge into the abyss. Then came the 'fashion creators', designers who didn't come from the world of *haute couture*. Nobody would disagree that today it is they that are both creative and talented and that the future lies in their hands. But let us return to Saint Laurent. His creative output over nearly forty years has been made up of echoes, ruptures and allusions made in connivance and complicity with women. He has always believed that clothes should be at the disposal of women and not the other way round. He has invented his own immediately recognizable vocabulary, syntax and grammar. A dazzling and uncontested colourist, he has brought his art to the frontiers of painting and drawn inspiration from Mondrian, Picasso, Braque, Matisse, Warhol and Wesselmann, not to forget Goya and Velasquez. But, as always with Saint Laurent, there has never been any question of mere copying. On the contrary, these painters enabled him to reinvent a language which has become his own. Warhol knew this, and held Saint Laurent in great esteem.

Yves Saint Laurent had begun to keep company with artists many years earlier when he discovered his passion for the theatre. This passion was in reality born when, at the age of thirteen, he saw a performance of Molière's *Ecole des femmes* directed by Louis Jouvet with sets and costumes by Christian Bérard. That day dream became reality. Yves had been given a lesson, he had listened and understood. The great lesson that Jouvet and Bérard had given him without knowing it was that of universal theatre, that of art. Everyone knows that there is nothing more false than reality nor more deceptive, yet when fiction embraces the mysteries of creation, no longer attempting to slavishly imitate reality but simply to suggest it, it becomes more real than reality. This is what Madeleine Renaud means when she writes: 'Yves Saint Laurent has the genius of a poet and when he dresses a body its soul appears.'

Yves Saint Laurent is a classic figure. One should be wary of such people. He is first and foremost an artist, that is to say a revolutionary. An anarchist without knowing it, without wanting to be one, he has remained subversive throughout his career. His contempt for all that is bourgeois, rather like Flaubert's, has fired his love for those to whom he has always felt close: the true aristocracy possessed of discernment and elegance and the faceless millions who wear his clothes. Both owe him a great deal. Long gone is the day when the timid young man from Oran submitted his sketches for Christian Dior's approval. Today that young man has become a universally respected master. Of course there will be others – some have already arrived – but let us not indulge in the absurd pseudo-Freudian game which would have us kill the father so that the children may live. Yves Saint Laurent's contribution is irrefutable. Just as he owes a great deal to those that came before him, Dior, Chanel, Balenciaga, Schiaparelli, Vionnet, those to come will owe him an undeniable tribute.

today, at the age of sixty, Yves Saint Laurent can stand back and observe the work he has accomplished. Looking over his shoulder he may catch a glimpse of that teenage boy who dreamt of glory. He can at last stretch out his hand towards him and show him that beyond glory there lies another truth, that of the ultimate confrontation between the creator and his creation.

as for those of us who have witnessed this fabulous destiny unfold day after day, how better can we do it justice than by quoting Nabokov? 'We watch the artist build his house of cards and watch the house of cards become a castle of gleaming steel and glass.'

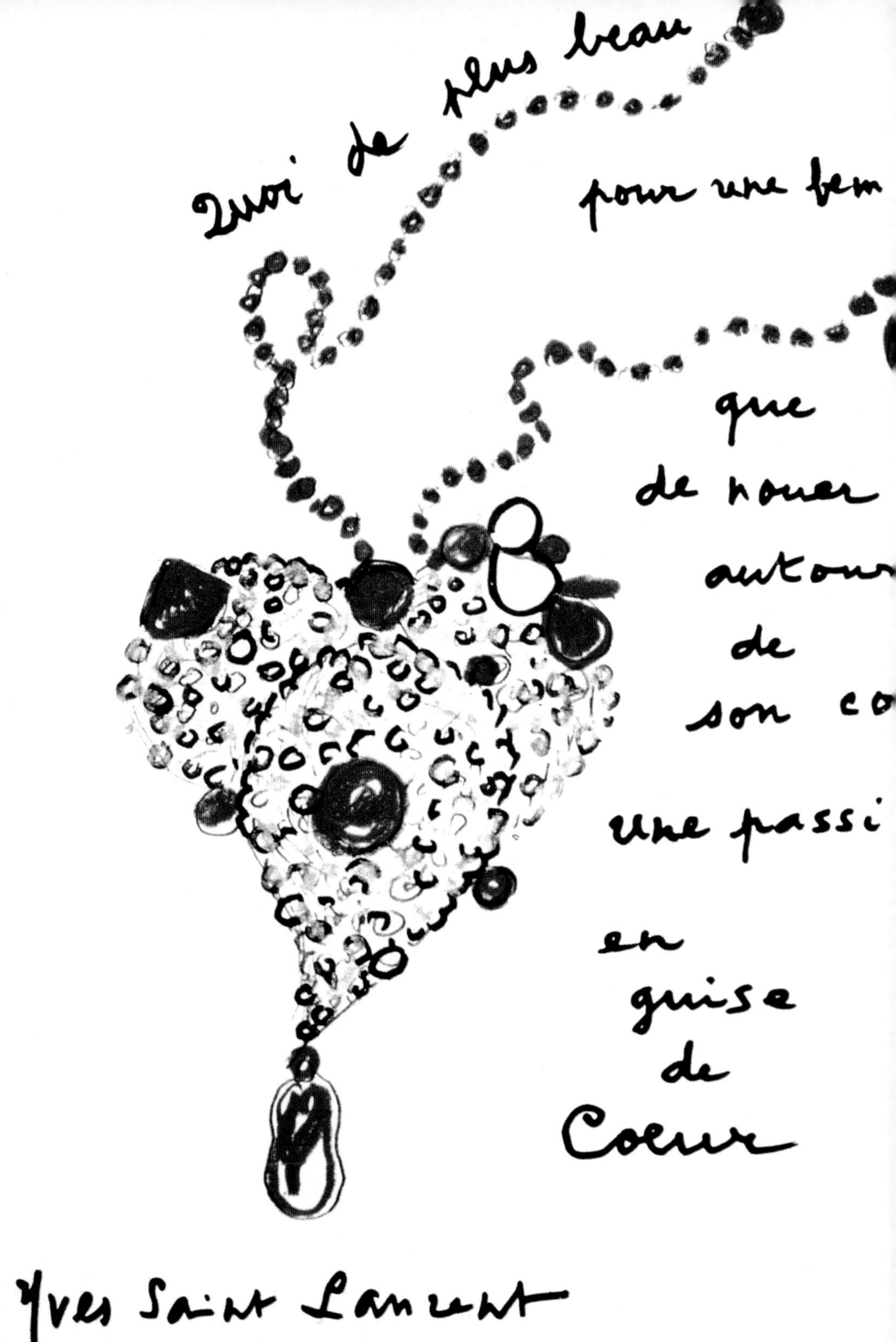

Quoi de plus beau

pour une fem

que

de nouer

autour

de

son co

une passi

en

guise

de

Coeur

Yves Saint Laurent

Chronology

1936   1 August, Yves Saint Laurent born in Oran, Algeria, where he spends his youth.

1954   Moves to Paris, where he attends the school run by the Chambre Syndicale de la Haute Couture and wins the top award of the International Wool Secretariat.
He is introduced to Christian Dior who immediately takes him on as an assistant.

1957   Following the death of Christian Dior, Yves Saint Laurent is chosen as his successor.

1958   Yves Saint Laurent wins the Fashion Oscar from Neiman Marcus.

1959   First designs of theatre costumes (*Cyrano de Bergerac*, ballet by Roland Petit).

1961   With Pierre Bergé, founds the Yves Saint Laurent couture house.

1962   29 January, Yves Saint Laurent presents his first collection under his own name.

1964   Yves Saint Laurent creates 'Y', his first perfume for women.

1966   First 'smoking'.
Opening in Paris of his first *prêt-à-porter* boutique, Saint Laurent Rive Gauche.
Yves Saint Laurent is named top fashion designer by *Harper's Bazaar*.

1967   Éditions Tchou publishes Yves Saint Laurent's strip cartoon, *La Vilaine Lulu*.

1968   First appearance of the safari look.

1969   Opening in Paris of the boutique Saint Laurent Rive Gauche pour Hommes.

1971   The Summer 1971 'Forties' collection creates a furore.
Launch of the perfume 'Rive Gauche' and of Yves Saint Laurent's first perfume for men, 'Pour Hommes'.

1973   Costume designs for Maïa Plissetskaïa in Roland Petit's ballet *La Rose malade*, for Colin Higgins's *Harold et Maude*, for Jeanne Moreau, Delphine Seyrig and Gérard Depardieu in Peter Handke's *La Chevauchée sur le lac de Constance*, and for Roland Petit's ballet *Schéhérazade*.

1975   Launch of the perfume 'Eau libre'.

1976   Acclaim for the 'Ballets Russes' collection.

1977   Creation of the perfume 'Opium'.

Winter 1992. Yves Saint Laurent aims to shock with this dress of faille and black velvet which leaves the breasts exposed, under a light veiling of organza. Photo: David Seidner.

1981	Creation of the perfume 'Kouros', for men. Creation of Marguerite Yourcenar's costume for her entry into the Académie française.
1982	Yves Saint Laurent receives the International Award of the Council of Fashion Designers of America, coinciding with the celebrations for the twentieth anniversary of his couture house.
1983	Creation of the perfume 'Paris'. Retrospective at the Metropolitan Museum of Art in New York: 'Yves Saint Laurent – 25 Years of Design'. This is the first time the museum has so honoured a living designer.
1985	A second retrospective is staged at the Palace of Fine Arts, Beijing: 'Yves Saint Laurent 1958–1985'. Yves Saint Laurent is awarded the Légion d'honneur, and a few months later receives the Fashion Oscar.
1986	Major retrospective: 'Yves Saint Laurent, 28 années de création', at the Musée des Arts de la Mode in Paris and the newly opened Tretiakov Gallery in Moscow. Yves Saint Laurent is appointed as a senior adviser to the government of the People's Republic of China.
1987	Exhibition 'Yves Saint Laurent, 28 années de création' at the Hermitage Museum, Leningrad, and the Art Gallery of New South Wales, Sydney, Australia.
1990	Opening in Paris of the first boutique selling the range of Yves Saint Laurent accessories. Yves Saint Laurent exhibition at the Sezon Museum of Art, Tokyo.
1992	Celebrations at the Opéra Bastille, Paris, to mark the thirtieth anniversary of the house of Saint Laurent. Opening of the Yves Saint Laurent Institut de Beauté, in Paris.
1993	Launch of the new perfume for women, 'Champagne'. Presentation of the one hundred and twenty-fourth collection designed by Yves Saint Laurent. Exhibition 'Yves Saint Laurent – Exotismes' at the Musée de la Mode, Marseilles.
1995	Creation of the perfume for men, 'Opium'.
1996	Yves Saint Laurent presents his seventieth collection under his own name.

Glamorous and frivolous, flattering and flirtatious, feathers have always been an Yves Saint Laurent favourite. Among his preferred materials are bird of paradise, ostrich and cock feathers. A silk organza 'foundation' is created from sketches, the trimming of which is then entrusted to André Lemarié, the only specialist in Paris. Naomi wears a dress of bird-of-paradise feathers from the Winter 1987 collection. Photo: Claus Ohm. © Archives YSL.

Theatre

Revues and shows starring Zizi Jeanmaire (1961, 1963, 1970, 1972), sets and costumes.
Les Chants de Maldoror and *Rhapsodie espagnole* (Roland Petit, 1962), sets and costumes.
L'Aigle à deux têtes (Jean Cocteau, 1978), sets and costumes.
Cher menteur (Jérôme Kilty, adapted by Jean Cocteau, 1980), sets and costumes.

Costumes for:
Cyrano de Bergerac after Edmond Rostand (Roland Petit, 1959).
Les Forains (Roland Petit, 1961).
Le Mariage de Figaro by Beaumarchais and *Il faut passer par les nuages* by François Billetdoux (Renaud-Barrault company, 1964).
Adage et variation and *Notre-Dame de Paris* after Victor Hugo (Roland Petit, 1965).
Des Journées entières passées dans les arbres by Marguerite Duras (Renaud-Barrault company, 1965).
Les Monstres sacrés (Arletty's wardrobe; Jean Cocteau, 1966).
Délicate balance (*A Delicate Balance*) by Edward Albee (Renaud-Barrault company, 1967).
L'Amante anglaise by Marguerite Duras (Madeleine Renault's wardrobe; directed by Claude Régy, 1968).
Revues and shows starring Zizi Jeanmaire (1968–1977).
Sylvie Vartan shows (1970, 1972).
Johnny Halliday show (1971).
La Rose malade and *Schéhérazade* (Roland Petit, 1973).
Harold et Maude (*Harold and Maude*) by Colin Higgins (Madeleine Renault's wardrobe; Renaud-Barrault company, 1973).
La Chevauchée sur le lac de Constance by Peter Handke (directed by Claude Régy, 1973).
Ingrid Caven recital (1978).
Wings by Arthur Kopit (directed by Claude Régy, 1980).
Savannah Bay (Marguerite Duras, 1983).

Cinema

Costumes for:
Moira Shearer (*Black Tights*, Terence Young, 1960).
Claudia Cardinale (*The Pink Panther*, Blake Edwards, 1964 [designs: 1962]).
Sophia Loren (*Arabesque*, Stanley Donen, 1966 [designs: 1965]).
Catherine Deneuve (*Belle de jour*, Luis Buñuel, 1967; *La Chamade*, Alain Cavalier, 1968; *La Sirène du Mississippi*, François Truffaut, 1969).
Annie Duperey (*Stavisky*, Alain Resnais, 1974).
Helmut Berger (*The Romantic Englishwoman*, Joseph Losey, 1975).
Ellen Burstyn (*Providence*, Alain Resnais, 1977 [designs: 1976]).

Venice. Yves Saint Laurent created the sets and costumes
for the Zizi Jeanmaire revue at the Casino de Paris in 1972.
© Archives YSL.

1958. **Triumph for Yves Saint Laurent** at the age of twenty-one with his first collection at Dior, featuring the 'trapeze' look. In 1961 he was to open his own fashion house. Photo: Dalmas. © Sipa Press.
The first dress to appear under the Yves Saint Laurent label was designed for Mrs Arturo Lopez Willshaw in 1961. © Archives YSL.

January 1962, Yves Saint Laurent's first collection under his own name. Yves Saint Laurent and Pierre Bergé made all their preparations in the workrooms of the old Manguin couture house, rented for the occasion. Just two days before the show they moved to 30 bis rue Spontini, formerly the home of the painter Forain. The collection was rapturously received, heralding a glittering future for Yves Saint Laurent. Photo: Pierre Boulat. © Cosmos.

Winter collection 1962. Black wool dress with front draping. Photo: Pottier. © *L'Officiel*.
Winter 1963, the 'Robin Hood' collection revolutionized *haute couture*: black oilskin waterproof and black suede tunic, with leather hood and crocodile thigh boots. © All rights reserved.

In 1962, Cassandre designed the Yves Saint Laurent logo, soon to be recognized all over the world. © Archives YSL.
The see-through dress, as it was dubbed in America. The transparent look bares all but reveals nothing: long dress of black chiffon trimmed with ostrich feathers, with narrow belt in the form of a gold snake. Winter 1968. © All rights reserved.

Winter 1966. Jean Shrimpton in pageboy outfit inspired by Little Lord Fauntleroy. Knickers and jacket of black velvet, collar of white guipure. Shoes by Roger Vivier for Yves Saint Laurent. *Vogue Paris*, August 1965. © Photo: Guy Bourdin.
In 1965, the bride appeared in an ivory cocoon of knitted wool with satin ribbons, suggesting a Russian doll. Yves Saint Laurent always allowed his humour and imagination free rein for the bridal ensemble. Photo: Fouli Elia. © Scoop/*Elle*.

Paris pink. Long evening dress of black velvet and pink satin. Photo: Gilles Tapie. © Scoop/*Elle*.
The Saint Laurent couture house at 5 avenue Marceau. Photo: Sacha. © Archives YSL.

The 'Forties' collection of 1971 created a sensation with outfits such as this lace-backed cocktail dress of black crêpe. Jeanloup Sieff's 'bare-backed dress' is a classic of fashion photography. © Photo: Jeanloup Sieff.
1968, first collection for Saint Laurent Rive Gauche pour Hommes: black leather coat worn by Yves Saint Laurent. © Photo: Jeanloup Sieff.

Love. For every New Year since 1970, Yves Saint Laurent has designed his own greetings card to send to friends and members of the press. © Archives YSL.

'Pop art' collection, photographed in 1966 by Jean-Claude Sauer to illustrate the 'swinging sixties'.

Winter 1966, 'Pop art' collection inspired by Andy Warhol, Lichtenstein and Wesselmann. To celebrate twenty years of Yves Saint Laurent, Catherine Deneuve poses for Helmut Newton in this 'nude look' dress of black, purple and pink wool. © Photo: Helmut Newton.
Confidante, muse and right-hand-woman, Loulou de la Falaise possesses that indefinable Yves Saint Laurent look. Photo: J.-P. Maclet. © Archives YSL.

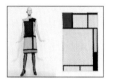

Winter 1965, 'Mondrian' collection. Yves Saint Laurent pays tribute to the painter Mondrian by using reproductions of his paintings on straight jersey dresses: 'Contrary to what people may think, the severe lines of the paintings matched the female body very well.' The first of many fruitful 'collaborations' with art and artists. © Archives YSL.
Mondrian painting, 1921, collection of Yves Saint Laurent and Pierre Bergé. © ABC.

Winter 1979, 'a tribute to Serge Diaghilev and his collaboration with Picasso' was how Saint Laurent explained this collection in a programme note. Short evening dress of black velvet and orange moiré with multicoloured satin appliqué. Photo: Duane Michals. © Archives YSL.
Spring/Summer 1969. Patchwork skirt in multicoloured silk and organdie blouse with flower print. © All rights reserved.

Summer 1967, 'African' collection. The acclaimed 'Bambara' dresses marked a complete break with the conventions of *haute couture*. For the first time, raffia and flax were used with wooden and glass bead embroidery. Photo: Claude Guegan. © *L'Officiel.*
In 1968, Veruschka poses in the famous laced safari jacket of beige cotton, worn with a belt of bronze rings and bermuda shorts of black cotton. An Yves Saint Laurent classic for day or evening wear. © Photo: Franco Rubartelli.

Masculine–feminine. The ambiguity is captured by Helmut Newton in 1975: trouser suit of anthracite wool with blouse of pearl-grey marocain crêpe. Trousers have been an essential item of the modern woman's wardrobe since first featured by Saint Laurent in 1966. © Photo: Helmut Newton.
Yves Saint Laurent photographed by Jeanloup Sieff in 1972. © Photo: Jeanloup Sieff.

Metal and floating veils: the collection of Winter 1969 is a marriage of modern sculpture and *haute couture*. Body sculpture by Claude Lalanne in golden-galvanized copper. © Photo: Manuel Litran.

Summer 1990. The 'Hommage à ma maison' jacket, embroidered in rock crystal by François Lesage, represents seven hundred hours of work. © Photo: Keiichi Tahara.
Summer 1989: bolero of gazar trimmed with *passementerie*, crystal and jade. © Photo: Bettina Rheims.

Van Gogh's sunflowers. It took 350,000 sequins, 100,000 ceramic bugle beads, all individually sewn, and six hundred hours of work to produce this sunflower-embroidered jacket by François Lesage, who worked from Yves Saint Laurent's design. © Archives Lesage.

Summer 1988, the 'Cubist' collection: cape in sand-coloured wool embroidered with motifs suggestive of Cubist collages. Shown here is Yves Saint Laurent's original sketch, together with the toile, which he also painted – these are the two indispensable stages through which every model must pass. © Sketch: Archives YSL and © Photo: François Halard.

Saint Laurent's heart mascot: design for the pendant encrusted with diamonds, rubies and pearls created by the couturier for his first collection, on 29 January 1962. It has featured at the close of every subsequent couture and *prêt-à-porter* collection, symbolizing his love of women. © Archives YSL.
Winter 1996. Yves Saint Laurent offers his heart to Stella. Evening coat of sable and black velvet with tunic embroidered with black sequins. © Photo: Claus Ohm.

Yves Saint Laurent's wedding gowns are the culmination not only of the show but of a particular passion or theme, be it Shakespeare, Verdi or Velázquez, Manet, Mozart or Scarlett O'Hara. Here Mounia poses with her cortège wearing the dress of iridescent purple and black faille from the Winter 1981 collection. © Photo: Arthur Elgort.

Costume for Zizi Jeanmaire. 'Pink champagne', Théâtre National de Paris, 1970. Yves Saint Laurent has designed many sets and costumes for the theatre, most notably for Roland Petit. © Photo: Jeanloup Sieff.
'The Sultan', costume designed for Jorge Lago in the Zizi Jeanmaire revue directed by Roland Petit at the Casino de Paris in 1972. © Photo: Jeanloup Sieff.

Inspiration and refuge: Morocco, and Marrakesh in particular, occupy an important position in Yves Saint Laurent's life and work. The Menara, photographed by Sacha. © Archives YSL.
Yves Saint Laurent's house in Marrakesh. © Photo: Marianne Haas.

Winter 1976, 'Ballets Russes–Opéra' collection: Cossack coats trimmed with mink, lavishly embroidered vests, multicoloured 'babushka' dresses, gypsy skirts with gold piping and diaphanous blouses. This collection was a huge international success, described on the front page of the *New York Times* as a 'revolutionary' collection 'that will change the course of fashion around the world'. © Photo: Guy Bourdin.

Hats. Yves Saint Laurent is one of the last couturiers to manufacture hats in his own atelier. Diptych of mirror images by David Seidner. Summer 1985 collection. © Photo: David Seidner.

Long evening dress in black velvet and white crêpe, photographed in 1982 by Horst. © Photo: Horst.
Summer 1990, a tribute to Rita Hayworth with this duffle-coat of black gazar worn over a black satin bodice and black 'smoking' trousers. © Photo: Keiichi Tahara.

The Yves Saint Laurent suit. Elegant and feminine, it has undergone many variations since 1962. Sporty or sophisticated, fitted or fluid, the aim is always for perfection and purity of line. This suit of grey whipcord and blouse of silver-grey satin, from Winter 1981, is photographed by Helmut Newton. © Photo: Helmut Newton.
Yves Saint Laurent Rive Gauche. Trouser suit in wool pinstripe. Summer 1995. © Photo: Mario Testino.

Saint Laurent classics. 'Grain de poudre' evening ensemble, or 'smoking'; sequin-embroidered sheath dress; two-piece suit; 'smoking' evening dress; cocktail dress of velvet and cock feathers. Photo: Jean-Marie Perier. © Scoop/*Elle*.

Yves Saint Laurent and the portraits of him painted by Andy Warhol in 1972. © Photo: Jeanloup Sieff.

Chronology and captions translated by Jane Brenton

The publishers wish to thank the Maison Yves Saint Laurent and most particularly M. Yves Saint Laurent, M. Pierre Bergé, Mme Loulou de la Falaise, Mlle Clara Saint, Mme Dominique Deroche, Mme Isabelle de Courrèges, Mlle Éléonore de Musset and Mlle Gaëlle d'Orange.

We are also indebted to Mme Catherine Deneuve, Alexis Gregory, François Baudot, Veruschka, Jean Shrimpton, Stella Tennant, Sybille Buck, Nadja Auermann, Marina Schiaro, Mounia, Naomi Campbell, Helmut Newton, Jeanloup Sieff, David Seidner, Horst, Pierre Boulat, Sacha, Bettina Rheims, Mario Testino, Jean-Marie Perier, Keiichi Tahara, Gilles Tapie, Fouli Elia, Marianne Haas, Manuel Litran, Duane Michals, Jean-Pierre Maclet, Claude Guegan, Jean-Claude Sauer, Claus Ohm, Franco Rubartelli and Samuel Bourdin.

Finally, this book could not have been published without the help and cooperation of Angela (TDR), François (Sipa Press), Jean Tissier (*L'Officiel*), Sylvianne (Scoop), Karine (Absolu), Didier (Élite) and Suzanne Dalton. Our thanks to them all.